CW00545659

The Christmas Candle Book

with poems of light by
Rosemerry Wahtola Trommer

RED ROCK PRESS

ISBN: 0-9714372-5-4

Published by Red Rock Press
New York, New York
U.S.A.

www.RedRockPress.com

Trommer, Rosemerry Wahtola
Celebration: The Christmas Candle Book: with poems of light / by
Rosemerry Washotla Trommer. P. cm.
ISBN: 0-9714372-5-4
1.Christmas-Poetry. 2. Candle-Poetry. 3. Light-Poetry 1. Title.
PS3570.R5875C45 2004
811í.6(dc22

2003027963

Printed in Singapore

COVER AND BOOK DESIGN: INKSTONE DESIGN, INC.

Introduction

When I was a girl, our family prepared for Christmas by lighting four candles in an advent wreath. Mom made the wreath from pinecones she'd found in the Wisconsin woods. To brighten it up, she tucked in loops of pink and purple velvet ribbon.

Our ritual took place each night before bedtime. We turned off all the living room lights and circled around the wreath. My younger brother and I took turns lighting the tapers. To light the candles was a great privilege.

The first week of Advent, we lit a purple candle, which symbolized hope. The second week, we added another purple candle, this one for peace. The pink candle (my favorite) was added in the third week—it stood for joy. And the final week (Christmas was so close!) we lit a purple candle, and prayed for love—for God so loved the world He gave His only son. Each week as the light increased, so did our excitement.

Except for birthdays, Christmas was the only time my family burned candles. I came to associate their light with pleasure, gifts, family, prayer and incredible anticipation.

The Egyptians are credited as the first to dip rushes into animal fat, enabling it to burn longer. The Romans first used wicks. Like the Egyptians, they made tallow candles, using them for evening travel and worship.

These early candles were practical, making the warmth and light of fire portable; however, there's nothing romantic about tallow. It smokes profusely, smells putrid, and drips freely—all for a feeble glow. At least tallow was cheap.

Not until the Middle Ages did people make candles from beeswax, the clear substance bees secrete when building honeycomb. It burns clean, smells pleasant, and doesn't drip much. But for centuries it was so costly that only churches used it.

Imagine being alive then: living in a dark, non-electric world, stepping into a church filled with beeswax candlelight. Bees themselves were considered symbols of purity, and the candles from their wax were like the candles of my childhood—heralds of something important, wonderful and mysterious.

Though the candle is commonplace these days, it still presents us with an opportunity to marvel. Like Christmas itself, each candle is a promise: No matter how dark, how cold, how bitter the world may be, even the tiniest light makes a difference.

—ROSEMERRY WAHTOLA TROMMER
  Telluride, Colorado

A Very Merry Christmas

With every kind wish at this holiday season. May the New Year bring you Happiness and Good Luck.

Assurance for When the Nights Are Long

Tonight, let's burn candles, count stars,

go for walks holding hands with the moon.

Let's start wildfires in the woods of our minds.

Tomorrow, dance with me wildly at noon

when the sun crowns the sky.

It's ours to collect, this wealth of radiance.

To chase out the dark, we need only a glimmer to start.

Friendly Christmas Wishes

May the atmosphere at Christmas
Of cozy warmth and cheer
Pervade your home and fill your heart
With happiness this year!

Glad Tidings

Advent

Evenings I watch the candle's orange flame
leap up from the wick to lick the dim room.

Mothlike, my eyes fixate on the light.
They can find no other place to land.

Wiser men than I have journeyed many miles
for a radiance, longing to believe in its promise.

I shut my eyes and the flickering remains
a merry glow that pervades even what is closed.

Permeable. Summoning. Brilliant. Alive.
Spirit, be like that in me.

For God So Loved the World

Even into the darkest thoughts,
faith gallops,
like white-muscled horses bearing holiness.
There is nowhere
that heaven can't shine.

Starter Angel

This is the perfect starter angel
for children who've never
had a guardian angel before.
Though she looks young,
don't be fooled by cherubic cheeks.
In Angel Years, Celestina
is over 2,000 years old
and has vast experience
creating butterflies and balls
that entice toddlers away
from busy intersections.
She makes the tap water stop
before the bathtub overflows
and will provide bright moonlight
anytime the nightlight bulbs burn out.
A perfect Christmas present
for children ages 2-6.
No assembly required.

Frohe Weihnachten
und ein glückliches Neues Jahr

SWEDEN, 1911

Newsworthy

The news tonight is that a miracle is happening.

For though winter has scoured the warmth from the days,

and thick clouds have covered Orion's jeweled belt,

the sun still drapes it's ruby mantle across the west,

as if a wee old man has lit ten thousand candles

just past the horizon, and all the childlike wonder

you thought you'd forgotten beats wild against your breast.

Candle Logic

As we migrate
from the realm

of substance to spirit
may we fuel our passage

with lit intention,
tendering everything we are,

exuding warmth,
absorbing prayer,

joining the whole
as we disappear

Just Checking

I've been too busy with Christmas to see it—
scurrying mouse-like to get everything done:

Wrap the presents? Check. Buy the eggnog? Check.
Mail the cards? Bake the cookies? Check. Check.

I'm checked out.

How could I shutter myself so completely?
Even a mouse stops to savor the tiniest crumbs.

What if I said, "To heck with my checklist?"
You guessed it: The Christmas spirit still comes.

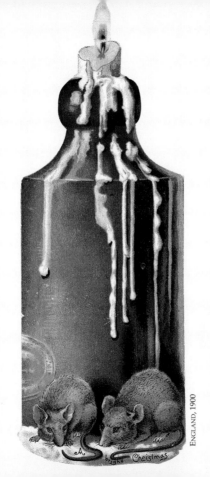

A bright Christmas

ENGLAND, 1900

ITALY

Creed

The candle flame stammers,
then sings through the pane,
pushing back the boundaries
of darkness, and night returns
to where it was. I believe in
night, in hand-dipped candles
that drip onto sills, in Orion,
in the frost that fills windows
and the sun that returns the
frost to the air. I believe in
Christmas, in moon, in stars
so bright that we follow them
to birthplaces, mothers who
love their children, children
who jump like live sparks
around the tree, and gifts
that can not be opened, only
received. These are the things
I would give you: this darkness,
this light, this all that is.

Humility

The candle needs no praise.
It quietly burns until all is consumed,
scrubbing the darkness from the room.

U.S.A.

Christmas Eve

Tonight, we are wild, half-drunk on candlelight,
and giddy as the swirling flame.

Inside, I feel young again.
I want to run toward morning

and unwrap all its gifts,
then play till I drop in a joyful heap.

Who could sleep?
The night giggles with promise

and each moment feels
like the present.

Encircled

Whenever you meet a stranger in winter,
whether you're shuffling through slush,
or slouched in a plastic seat on the bus,
lift up your gaze from below your cap
to look in his eyes for the tiny candle
that you've heard poets speak of,
some glimmer of humor or honeyed delight
that re-ignites when we greet each other,
spreading its light into concentric circles,
ever widening. Imagine a rush hour bus
aglow inside from the tiny candles in all of us,
each one relit by someone who dared to look up
and smile at another instead of just looking away—
seeing at last not another brown coat in a seat,
but a human, illuminated, a sliver of divinity.

Greetings

U.S.A.

Silly Old Wives' Tale

Said the one wee man,
"Why shouldn't we dance 'round the candlelit tree
with swinging elbows and bouncing knees
singing hee hee hee like calliopes?
It's Christmas Eve! It's a jubilee!"

Said the other wee man,
"You're right my friend. Though my wife will scold
that I'll catch cold and my knees are old
our blessings here are manifold!"
So they did a quick jig round the candle's gold.

Well, yes, the next day,
The man's legs stiffened like two silver fifes
And he sniffed with a cold—worst one of his life.
His Christmas Day was full of aches and strife,
And he said, "From now on, I'll listen to my wife."

Remembering How
to Pray

In the curling dim hush
of candlelight mass
anything seems possible.

Though the limbs are now stiff
as hardened wax, the lips recall carols
from Christmases past

and forgotten prayers start to leap up
like the candle's white flame,
ecstatic and willing, filling the night.

Glædelig Jul og Godt Nytaar

The Daughter's New Clothes

Dark blue velvet, the dress you stitched for me,
with a white eyelet bib and a rounded lace collar.

I wore it once for midnight Christmas mass, kneeling
between you and Dad, holding a thin white candle in a cup.

That night, I felt like a gift, something treasured and worthy,
wrapped with intention and offered with love to the world.

I grew out of the dress two months after you made it,
the shoulders too tight, the new plastic zipper reluctant.

As my sleeve lengths stretched out and inseams matured,
you knit me a coat of prayers I couldn't grow out of, only grow into.

And wearing it now with its cuffs just right, I feel like a present,
wrapped with your warm intention and offered with love to the world.

A Merry Christmas to you.

Russia, circa 1910

CHRISTMAS GREETINGS

'Twas the Night

Would you wait up all night
for a man who promised
to give you everything
you want?
All you have to do is be good.
You tell the children, "Please go to sleep."
But propped up on couch pillows, you wait.
Would you recognize him
if you saw him?
Too soon the wait is over.
Sunlight squeezes through the window.
On the table
the four red sugar cookies
you set out for him.
One by one,
you eat them,
the sweetness sings in your mouth.
Hair unbrushed, squealing,
the kids run-tumble-skip down the stairs,
and you realize
you have everything
you want.

She Was Alone For Christmas

It was cold.
Outside,
icicles hung
in the window.
Inside,
the woman
lit four golden candles.
Beeswax blazed
through the room
like laughter.
The night outside
shivered.

The woman's skin
glowed.
Joy is
our birthright.
When the sun rises
even the icicles
melt into music.
Even the night
is warmed
into light
by the stars.

Invitation

Don't worry that the night is long.
Build a fire, burn a candle,
hug your children, say a prayer.

Warmth is there for the making.
There are ten thousand ways
to tender the light.

Inside this Christmas Candle

That which has been created can never be destroyed.
—West African Prayer

Inside this Christmas candle sings the memory of June
and dizzy bees traipsing between purple clover
before buzzing back to their hive, drunk on nectar.

And, oh! the gold in their cool, busy comb,
where the bees gorge on honey, make wax in their bodies
then sculpt the white flecks into a home.

Their honeycomb walls now feed this thin wick,
and their wax glints like sunshine through winter solstice.

I'LL welcome joyous Christmas,
And hail the new born year.
For all that brings thee pleasure.
To me is doubly dear.

LONDON.

ENGLAND, 1880

For My One
Who Is Gone at Christmas

Once I wanted to give you everything,
ten thousand chocolate truffles,
books with happy endings,
and new black socks without holes in the toes.

There is no beautiful box
that can hold what I want for you now—

to gather you into the warm ring of my arms,
to give you a candle that burns bright as love,
and to bring you home, home, home, bring you home.

Guidance

This happiness wavers inside me
like a candle flame
whipped by the breeze,
at one moment dazzling,
distilling the gold from the air,
the next moment forked and flickering
a sputter of doubt,
more black smoke than flame.

You have felt it, too,
haven't you?
The shudder when the air itself betrays you,
the miracle when the light,
wild with wind,
stills again,
a beacon in your body,
leading you always,
through the waves toward shore.

ST CHRISTMAS WISHES.

U.S.A., 1908

Christmas Greetings

The Gift

You have lit a candle
in me,
a tiny flame that shimmers
and though no one else sees it,
inside, I shine.

Miracle

Tonight I stare at the star-crowded sky
searching for something bright enough
to believe in, a place where faith sparkles
so clearly that I would walk across continents
to see what miracle breathes below it.

Over a billion stars embrace the universe
and six times more humans breathe below:
each of us miraculous, beloved, born to beam,
to praise, to forgive, to bring hope,
to spread love and to shed a little light.

U.S.A.

Merry Christmas to My Son

I'm wishing lots of Christmas fun,
And lots of Christmas joy
For you, who mean so much to me,
My own, dear Christmas boy

U.S.A.

Dear Santa,

Please give my son
all the things I'd like to buy him,
but can't.
I'll get him the football,
the clown doll that talks,
and the Game Boy
(even though the beep blip drives me nuts).
He wants a REAL giraffe, desperately.
Don't worry about that one.
But I'm counting on you, Santa,
to give him
a broader sense of wonder,
a belief that miracles happen,
a respect for all children,
and a longing to be good.
Please, Santa, bring him
the delight that comes from giving
without expecting.
And Santa, for my stocking,
please, bring me the same thing.

Strands

The winter nights are so long now
that every tiny sliver of light glitters
like a promise that darkness won't always reign.

Let's gather small bits of candle flame,
star glimmer, snow crystals spiked with moon,
and let's link them together in our memories

like a long string of Christmas tree lights,
or perhaps like a luminous rosary—
a holy strand we can keep in our mind's back pocket.

Each glimmer or flash forms another bright bead of thanksgiving
a prayer we can rub through our shadowed thoughts,
repeating until the world glistens again.

With Sincere Wishes for Christmas
and the New Year

So Far Away

If the sun's light takes only eight minutes to reach Earth,
then when I light this candle,
how long will it take for my prayer to reach you?
And will you feel it—
like a soft glow that appears, quiet as morning,
or perhaps like the thick golden rays that clang noon?
And will you, perhaps, feel a wave of warmth,
as if someone just hugged you,
and whispered,
"Merry Christmas, I love you."
And just for a moment,
would it feel
as if darkness disappeared?

Sing Along

The song of the candle's flame
is silence.

Though I belt out boisterous fa la la la las
and carol merrily along

with the "Little Drummer Boy,"
"Oh Come Let Us Adore Him,"

and "Angels We Have Heard on High,"
my favorite lyric is the candle's song:

the repeating chorus of
silence   silence.

I smile wide at the bong bing ting of bells
and the swelling al-le-lu-ia of choirs

and the crackling snaps of aspen wood fire
that herald the Christmas time,

but my holiest hymn is the one
where stillness fills mouths, ears, will

and deep listening begins.

Vespers

The evening twirls
around the candle.
In my mouth,
a thousand thanks
swirl like hot cider,
then spiral out into
soft prayers.

I speak into the flame.
The light wavers,
and the room wildly spins
alive. Amen. I return
to stillness. The light
straightens its spine.
Everything shines.

U.S.A.

Resolution

The new year flares up
like a candle,
never lit,
its eager wick, still white,
tastes fire for the first time.

Each resolution ignites
like that zealous first light,
forecasting shadows,
creating an outline
of what we wish would be.

But the silhouette on the calendar's wall
is mere form without substance.
The texture and tone come
only by living,
letting the candle burn.

Christmas Greetings

A JO
CHRI

Eve

Tonight I am so in love with the world
that every hollow within me fills with light.

I burn like the morning star releasing the dawn,
like the thick-wicked candle feasting on air.

I am the bonfire's leap through each long winter night,
the flamboyant pearl swelling inside the dark clam.

After tonight, all that will be left of me is
a feathery sweep of gray ashes, dancing into daylight.

Merry Christmas!